YOU ARE A POWERFUL CREATOR

Creating Peace

Written by Monica Iglesias

Illustrated by Robert Paul Matheus
& Raul Ramirez

Based on actual events

Additional books can be ordered through

MonicaIglesiasAuthor.com, EmanateLove.com or Amazon.com.

DEDICATION

This book is dedicated to André - a true peacemaker.
Thank you for the gift you are to me in my life and to humanity.

PREFACE

As a parent, I thought I had to sacrifice everything for my children, apparently even my sanity. I felt that their happiness and success in life depended solely on me as their mother. That was a heavy burden to carry alone. I got burnt out a lot until I realized that I didn't have to do it all myself.

I learned how to empower the children in my stewardship to be conscious creators of happiness, peace, love, courage, joy and so much more, through a series of quality questions much like the ones highlighted in this book. I learned that their answers were inside of them all along. I didn't have to tell them what to do or how to be, I just needed to know how to guide them.

Empowering them has changed my life and released a heavy burden. Today, we co-create the life we choose to experience TOGETHER. I am so grateful for the powerful little creators in my life. They have taught me so much of what is possible for me in my own life and have inspired countless others.

After breakfast, the children scampered off to play, *giggling,* *laughing,* and making lots of noise!

Mother finally took a moment to sit down and rest. She had a busy and difficult week. She loved to see her children happy and joyful, but today she really wanted to relax and experience peace.

André noticed mother still in the kitchen and returned to see if she needed any help.

"Do you need anything, Mommy?" he asked.

Mother sighed and said, "I would really like to experience Peace today. **Would you assist me in creating Peace?"**

"Sure!" He said with a willing attitude.

"Do you know what peace feels like?" mother asked.

He thought about it for a moment, then shook his head and said, "Not exactly."

Then mother asked, "If you don't know what peace feels like, how could you find out?"

"Hmmm..." André thought.

"Who do you think might know?" mother inquired.

"Maybe I could ask the Angels or my Higher Power," he wondered out loud.

"That sounds like an excellent idea," mother agreed. "Where would be a good place to ask them?"

"In Nature?" he thought out loud. "Maybe I could go in the back yard."

"That's a wonderful idea!" mother agreed. "Let me know what you discover."

★ André went out into the backyard to be in nature.

★ He found a nice, comfortable, grassy spot on the hillside.

★ He sat down and took several deep belly breaths.

★ Then he quieted his mind.

★ He held the intention in his heart to discover what Peace felt like.

As he did this, the sounds of the traffic in the distance began to fade.

He closed his eyes, and began to be aware of everything around him.

He heard...

the birds chirping and singing in the distance.

He noticed...

the movement of the leaves in the trees.

He felt...

the wind brush across his skin and move through his hair.

When André opened his eyes everything seemed to be in slow motion. He noticed the details of the

blades of grass, the little bugs, and insects

crawling about.

He felt connected to everything, and as he did, he felt a

soft calm quiet feeling

enter his heart and his entire body.

He was amazed by what he felt and went inside
to tell his mother.

Mother noticed André return and asked,

"So, what does peace feel like?"

"It's a soft calm quiet feeling in my heart." he responded.

"Yes it is!" mother agreed. "That is a beautiful way to describe it."

"Now that you know what peace feels like," mother added, "What are some ways you can create peace in our home today?"

"We can do quiet activities," he began. "We can speak softly to each other. . . We can read a book and create win/wins so that the other person doesn't get upset and cry or yell." André was full of ideas.

"That sounds wonderful!" mother agreed. "Thank you for being willing to create peace today."

André continued to come up with ideas throughout the day to create peace. He inspired everyone around to speak and play peacefully together.

The older children even prepared food for the younger
children which allowed mother additional time
to rest, meditate, and rejuvenate.

When mother entered the living room she found each of the children reading a book. She sat next to André and said, "Wow! Look what a powerful creator you are! You inspired you brother and sisters to create peace by being calm, gentle, and loving with them. I feel so much peace, gratitude, and love in my heart for what you have created. Thank you!!!"

"You're welcome, mommy," André said with a smile on his face and an AMAZING feeling in his heart.

Mother thanked each child for their part in creating peace that day.

There are times when we are our children's teacher.
There are times when they are our teachers;
and there are times we are simply EQUALS.

Note to Parents:

10 Tips to Empower
The Children In Your Stewardship

1: **EXPRESS YOUR NEEDS** in a loving way. Be real! You have needs too. But avoid forcing the child to comply just because you are the "parent".

2: **ASK** the child for assistance in the form of a request. Avoid demanding, commanding or manipulating.

3: **GUIDE** the child to discover their answers through Quality Questions. Avoid "telling" them what to do.

4: **LET THEM KNOW** how much it would please you. Most children naturally want to please their parents. They just need to know how.

5: **EXPRESS GRATITUDE** for their willingness to help.

6: PRAISE THEM! If you don't feel that they were successful, swallow your criticism and celebrate their willingness to put forth the effort. Find something you can praise them for. If you criticise them, they may never want to try again.

7: RECEIVE THEIR ACT OF SERVICE as a true gift. Receive it as you would a diamond ring or a fancy sports car.

8: CONSIDER AN EQUAL ENERGY EXCHANGE for them. Be open and willing to create something that they may want to experience, such as time at the park, or quality time with you. This is not as a condition or manipulation for their actions - it is an equal energy exchange - call it Karma, if you wish.

9. DEBRIEF THE CHILD by asking questions like: What did you feel worked? What didn't work? How would you do it differently next time? (avoid suggesting or leading them to *your* answers. Let them come up with the answers on their own.)

10: CELEBRATE the powerful creator they are! Celebrate the powerful creator you are as a parent as well.

As you praise, build, and empower the children for their acts of service, they will be more willing to continue making these efforts to create beautiful situations in your home and family life... in school... and in the world.

- - Peace Quotes - -

"The Planet does not need more successful people. The Planet desperately needs more peacemakers, healers, restorers, storytellers, and lovers of all kind."
-- Dalai Lama

"Be the CHANGE You wish to See in the World!"

— Ghandi

"Peace is not something you wish for;
It's something you make,
Something you do,
Something you are,
And something you give away."
-- John Lennon

And just to clarify... "PEACE... does not mean to be in a place where there is no noise, trouble, or hard work. It means to be in the midst of those things and Still Be Calm In Your Heart."
-- Unknown

Other books in this Series:

Creating Happiness

Introduction to this series and the framework for empowering children

Creating Light

Topic: Overcoming fear and darkness.

About the Creators

Monica Iglesias
author

Monica is a mother of four, a wife, an inspirational children's book author, mentor, and intuitive guide. She grew up in southern Utah and has lived in Puerto Rico and France. She enjoys traveling, spending time with her family, learning new things and connecting with others. After transforming her own life from victim to powerful creator, Monica chooses to empower children, youth and adults alike by introducing powerful principles through her books, mentoring sessions, and online training courses. She desires to share with others the magic of the power within.

Raul was born in Lima Peru. He has always loved art and drawing. He studied at the National School of Bellas Artes in Lima where he studied drawing, painting and sculpture. Later in 1991 he moved to the United States where he studied graphic design at the Valencia College in Florida. He now resides in Utah with his wife and 2 daughters.

Raul Ramirez
illustrator

Robert was born and raised in Lima, Peru, but has made northern Utah his home for the past 16 years. He is the father of two boys. His passion is art in all it's forms and expressions including, painting, sculpting, murals, graphic and interior design.

Robert Paul Matheus
illustrator

96387655R00019